How to be a Tiger

Poems by
GEORGE SZIRTES

Illustrations by
Tim Archbold

Otter-Barry BOOKS

Contents

You Have a Body

You have a body.
You're not air.
You're not just anywhere,
you're THERE.
I suppose you might feel new with it,
wondering what you might do with it.

Those arms and legs
can be flung about.
You can walk
   or run
      or fall over
         FLAT
      which is, of course,
the problem with that.

You can breathe, you can gasp,
you can cough, sneeze or rasp.
You have fingers!
You can grasp!

And it's all yours
to do what you want with,
to turn right round or
face the front with.

Or mostly yours,
though some of it belongs
to your mum and dad
to remind them of the bodies
they once had.

And yet it's yours –
you'll see it grow
though not so that
you ever know.
It's fun, it's great,
something you learn to operate.
Just pinch yourself and see.
Who is that? It's YOU not me.

It's yours to wear and yours to be.
And it comes free!

Learning to Walk and Run

First
step

Sec-
ond
   step.

And a ten-
ta... tive   *third.*

And a fourth.

You bowl along
like a planet
not quite in control
of its orbit
like a comet
lurching
like a meteor
not yet

crashing.

Oh Mr Bear
Are you there?
Shall we run through the wood?
Shall we gallop through dead leaves? We should.
We should!

Oh Mrs Deer
Are you here?
Shall we pound across the lawn?
Shall we wake at dawn?
Yes! Let's do it!

Let's go on!

Running Poem

I discovered speed
by running as fast as I could.

If I could have run forever
I would.

Running isn't starting or stopping.
Running is what happens in between
when the world rushes by and you don't even notice
where you're going or where you've been.

You run and run and run
and nobody knows that you've begun.

I've begun. The wind is blowing.
I'll keep going.

Ladder

Climbing
a tree
is
difficult.

But you can
lean
a ladder
against it

and

scramble up
    like the little monkey you are.

Swing

The thing
   about a swing
      is the wing
   and spring
of it as you cling
      the fling
         and sting
     of air through your teeth
         as you breathe
     and the ground beneath
   rising and dropping
  coming and going
slowing, slowing

   stopping

stopping.

14

Talking Toddler Blues

First comes the cry.
You want to know why?

We want what we can't name.
We're scared or in pain
so we cry.

But slowly the sound
of the world all around us
doesn't merely astound us

No

It begins to mean
this and that
and that and this
it comes with a **growl**
it comes with a **hiss**
it comes with a **whoop**
in one continuous **loop**

then stops

and starts again,
nothing so plain
as a word,

what is heard
has to be unpicked
unsticked
exploded
decoded

and then one day
suddenly we say
something that sounds like the thing we hear
that hangs about our ear
and lodges there
in the brain
and again

and we say
mama
or *nana*
or *gaga*
or *haha*

a sound that is squeezed
and teased
and seized

and everyone's pleased.

Mooon

Mooon, says Marlie to the sky.

And there she is, the daylight moon
faint and curved and hardly there
but Marlie sees and points her out
and says the word as if it meant
something special not just air
glowing in a sky-blue tent.

Nor should there be any doubt
about that silver curving eye
looking back so neat and starly
as it winks back, *Hello, Marlie.*

Moon Music

That round clear sound you can hear
is the moon.
The gong that is struck in your ear
is the moon.
The song that the stars like to sing
is the moon.
The whistling sound of the bat's wing
is the moon.
The little bell that swings in the trees
is the moon.
The violin at night when your feet freeze
is the moon.
That mouth in the sky with the silver tongue
is the moon.
That squeaking-creaking woodwind in your lung
is the moon.
The tide as it rises and falls like a do-re-mi scale
is the moon.
Any music that is brilliant, cold and pale
is the moon.

Considering the Sun

Good morning, good morning!

Look, the sun is out.
Sometimes it is very grey
(sometimes it seems every day)
but this is sunlight, there's no doubt,
here's the sun – and it is out!

But if the sun is out just when
we call at its front door
how can it be shining now,
how can it slip across the floor,
how can it light the old flint wall,
how do anything at all
if it is out each time we call?

So is the sun in when it's out
or is it out when it is in?
I wish it would make up its mind,
my own mind is in such a spin
at what sun does and what it's done....

But never mind.

Good morning, sun!

Calling the Sun

I called the sun, I stood in line,
I rang its bell, asked it to shine.

Come out, sun!
Come out, sun!
COME OUT, SUN!

I said it three times like a spell
then once again I rang the bell.

RING!

And out it popped, the shiny thing.

It's Still Raining

Wet again,
yet again!
Down it drips,
little fingertips,
tapping
and snapping
as if the rain were cross.

See the branches toss?
See the puddles grow?
Has it stopped raining?

NO.

23

A Huge Wind

Listen to that wind!
Just listen to it *huff* and *puff*
(like the wolf in the story
with the three little pigs.)

Hold it there, wind!
That's enough.

But no!
The wind will blow
until it gets fed up of it
and nothing's going to get on top of it.

But the roof is tight
and the windows won't break.
So I'm saying good night....

The wind will be gone when I wake.

Running with the Wind

Whoosh! See
  how the branches bend
    and sway
      and the leaves
        fly like birds
          or rattle along the pavement
            strange scuttling creatures

Whoosh! See
  these words blow
    across the page
      almost off them
        in a sudden draught
          of speaking very fast
            as if your lungs were bursting

It is exhilarating
　　it makes you want
　　　　to run about like the wind
　　　　　　as if you were a small leaf
　　　　　　　　or a bird, or a strange
　　　　scuttling creature
　　　　　　　　　or a piece of paper
　　　like this,
　　　　　　　　settled,
　　　floating, then *blown*
　　　　　　　　　　right
　　　across the garden

Winter Sunlight

Look – the sun is out
but it's ever so shy.
It puts out its hand,
averting its eye.

It touches the wall,
but the patch is so small
it is pretty soon gone –
not for gazing on.

At this time of year
it doesn't appear
for too many hours

but when it does – it's ours!

Apes and Monkeys

Monkeys pull such silly faces
even the nicest are disgraces.

I once knew a Chimpanzee
who kept on chattering all through tea.

I once knew a Barbary Ape
who bent a teaspoon out of shape.

I once knew a Marmoset
who wrecked an entire dinner set.

I once knew a Tamarin
who threw my pudding in the bin.

I once knew a Colobus
who ate the cake, left none for us.

I once knew an Orangutan
who couldn't distinguish quiche from flan.

If you're expecting one for tea
get smart and take this tip from me –

shun apes and monkeys when you can.
Cancel! Or change the seating plan.

How to be a Tiger

The scary tiger roars and roars,
it slinks through shadows on all fours.
Children, beware! Are strange dogs howling?
No, it is the tiger growling.

The tiger growls, its eyes ablaze,
but we too have our tiger ways,
we too can pad through the dark wood
of the cosmic neighbourhood.

Pretend this is the forest floor.
Pad, tiger, pad! Now children,

ROAR!

33

The Bear in the Bathroom

There's a bear in the bathroom and a shark
    in the tub,
They are both out hunting, looking for grub.
Let's rub the magic lantern, rub-a-dub-dub!

There's an elk in the hallway and a crocodile
    in bed,
They're looking for their dinner if there's
    dinner to be had.
Let's pad quietly, pad-pad-pad!

There's a vulture in the kitchen and a dragon
    in the tower.
There's a wolf in the larder eating cauliflower.
Let's play it safe. Let's hide in the shower!

The animals are leaving, creep-creep-creep.
Time to go home now. Time to sleep.

Oleg the Meerkat

Meet our meerkat, Oleg
Yes he has one bow leg
But that's better than no leg
So come on Oleg, show leg

That's only your low leg
So low that is your toe leg
You have a lovely slow leg
A better-than-you-know leg

A leg with flow, a flow leg
A seven-at-one-blow leg
A real let-it-go leg
A fellow for your co-leg

A proud leg! Show it, Oleg.

The Cat and the Caterpillar

The cat sat on the lily pad
next to the caterpillar.
The caterpillar kept shuffling.
'I wish you'd sit there stiller,'
said the cat who'd never had
a companion on the lily pad.

A toadstool on the nearby bank
shook his head. *'Poor caterpillar.*
If you keep shuffling to and fro
you'll be the cat's next tummy-filler.'

Siblings

The day sits down,
night begins.
It is as though
the two were twins.

It is as though
sister and brother
had turned their backs
on each other.

Yours and Mine

Oh no you don't! This toy is mine!
If you want to use it, stand in line.

What's mine, what's yours, let's get it straight.
If you want mine you'll have to wait.

But if it is yours, well, I don't mind.
I just want a go. So please be kind.

It's not my house, it's not your house.
So give me that toy right now. OR ELSE!

Big Sister, Mother Tongue

Here's a word and here's another
Here's a sister and a brother
Here's the tongue that we call mother

Here's the world and here's what's not
Here's a bed that's not a cot
Here's a little that's a lot

Here's a baby's piercing cry
Here's the tear fresh from his eye
Here's the tired parents' sigh

Here's a baby on all fours
Here's my room and here is yours
Here's a house with all its doors

Hello world, here is my tongue
Neither too short nor too long
Just the right size for this song.

Waiting for School

Come on, Marlie, let's prepare,
Everything you could want is there...

Things to play with, things to learn,
Every child must take a turn.
Mummy, Daddy, went there too
When they were as young as you.

Oh but it's so big and tall!
Who'd want to be there at all?
The children may be fierce and wild.
And I am just a little child.

You say they work and then they play?

Then I might go – for just one day.

Teacher's Helper

Miss Faulks has a new helper called Miss Prime
Who follows Miss Faulks round most of the time.
Miss Faulks is patient, clever, neat and kind.
When she sits down Miss Prime sits down behind.
If I get lost Miss Faulks is sure to find me.
When I look round Miss Prime is just behind me.
Miss Faulks works hard, that's why Miss Prime must
    help her.

I too work hard. I sometimes need a helper.

Time to Learn

Put your hands up,
please don't shout.
If you want the loo,
ask to go out.
If you want my attention
wait your turn.
That's the first lesson.

Time to learn.

Spelling Your Name

Here's your name and how to spell it.
See it, hear it, touch it, taste it, smell it!

Beyond the letter, beyond the sound,
there is something that is you
captured in it, can you hear?
Listen closely
and wait for the name that is *you* to appear.

It's secret, it's a mystery
how any such name can stand in for a ME.

You didn't choose it
but we all use it –
and this is the sound we make when we call you.
We know you're not just this,
that it is not *all* of you.

But look, there it is in your pocket, in your hand
and in your eyes. It's clear you understand.
It's written down so it must be true.
We use those letters when we think of you.

That's you in writing, now you say it.
This is the game and you must play it.

Flying on Words

As you grow taller
Your sentences grow and grow.
You're no longer satisfied with *want*, *again*,
    and *no*.

Now you start adding parts of speech
Until sentences grow way beyond your reach.

Soon the language runs away with you,
and you're flying on words and it's like being
    dragged through
hedges backwards, time and again, but you
    have to keep talking, and so you do.

Oh what a chatterbox you are and you speak
    such wondrous stuff.
Have you had your say yet?

No, not enough.

How Long? How Far?

Look, we're getting in the car.

How long? How far?

Oh, many miles of road,
down boring motorways.
It's going to take *days*!

Not days but hours
that seem to c r e e p,
that are far too long,
that last for ever
till you sleep
and sleep some more
until they open the door
and you get out of the car

and

there you are!

Walking the Plank

Captain Hook says
WALK THE PLANK.
He's the boss,
he has the rank.

He can make Wendy, Michael and John,
Tinker Bell, Pan, The Lost Boys, and, need I go on...
yes, even Nana the Dog
walk that plank and go the whole hog.

Tread that plank then, but be brave –
the bedroom is no watery grave,
its icy waters are no shock,
the only danger a well-fed croc
waiting to dart with his *tick-tick-tock*
though he, as you'll know if you've read the book,
is only after one man, Hook!

And see, there's Hook, on the cold sea floor,
sneaking towards the bedroom door.

51

A Song for Captain Hook

Yo-ho-ho and scrub my back.
My blade is sharp, my heart is black.
And as for you, you scurvy crew,
I've seen burst tyres more fit than you.

Yo-ho-ho and boil my shirt.
You're quick to chat but slow to hurt!
Despite your roars and empty threats
You're Puss in Boots, mere household pets.

Yo-ho-ho and brush my teeth.
You're hard on top but soft beneath!
My gun is loaded, my breath foul,
And I can bellow. I can howl.

Yo-ho-ho and best beware.
When I breathe fire I fry the air!
I am a pirate, my cracked heart
Is where your troubles really start.

Yo-ho-ho and say your prayers.
It's time to wind up your affairs!
I'll play it rough, not by the book.
You're Peter Pan? Well,
                            I am
                                    HOOK!

Halloween

Whoo-whoo!

Who are you?

*I am the ghoul
you met in school!
Bring me treats,
that is the rule.*

*Don't run away!
Don't think to risk it!
Bring me cake
or bring me biscuit.*

Yummy yum!
The ghosts have come!
Now they've eaten
they move on!

ABRACADABRA!

They have gone!

54

How Old Are You Now?

Bang the drum and blow the horn.
You're born!

It's the biggest thing you've ever done!

Then time creeps up
  And then you're *one*,

    Then *two*,
      Then *three*,
        Then *four*,
            And then one more
            And more....

What excitement! All because of you!
How old are you again?

I thought you knew!

Money

What is money?
    coins and paper
    wallets and purses
    pockets and handbags
    slots and tills
    hats on the pavement.

How did it get here?
    someone has earned it
    someone has made it
    someone has kept it
    someone has spent it
    someone has lost it.

Give it and take it –
    buy what you need
    buy what you want
    buy what you dream of
    get it, exchange it
    get something solid
    get something dreamy.

What does it feel like?
little and heavy
crinkly and folded
sweaty and dirty
warm as your body
cold as the east wind.

In the Park: Autumn

A chill gust thrusts
the leaves one way then another.
The lady with the umbrella
billows past us like a blown leaf.

We are running on the path,
me and my brother.
We too might get blown away
with the leaves.

In the Park: Winter

Everything is frozen, especially me.
Those cold imps scrambling up my sleeve
and down my collar have mischief in mind.

The bare branches stand stiffly to attention.
My ears are like two wounds, red and raw.
Does winter have to be cruel to be kind?

In the Park: Spring

It is like the world in the morning,
suddenly very bright and startling.
Things bounce and blossom. It is
as if my fingers had turned into streams
of light and warmth. And there's the pond
with its ducklings. Too much of everything.

In the Park: Summer

Even the wind has grown lazy.
We are leisurely on the lawn, *la la*.
Can you hear singing? It's just the grass
pretending to sing. Maybe it's us.
Maybe we are turning into music.
Maybe we are lazy. Maybe we should sleep.

The Leaping Hare

Darts down the road,
Melts into grass, stock still,
Drums on the still moon,
Is hunted and, grey with age,
Leaps.   And is gone.

November Hare

The November hare
is neither here nor there.

As the cold squeezes in
it is where it's been

though it's hard to know where.

Rookery

Caw! goes the cry
Against the black sky
It's blacker than it looks
A cloud of black rooks
A flight of black devils
At their dusk revels
High *caw* and high *croak*
A plume of black smoke.

Swallows

Hunting on the wing
all billow and swoop
laughing as they go
pouring from the sky
in one vast troupe
they fly tails forked
suddenly uncorked

The Princess and the Bad King

The princess is bad.
The dragon is bad.
The king is bad.
The prince is bad.
Even the frog is bad.

Something is wrong.
Someone should be good,
if not the dragon
or the king,
the frog at least,
or the princess.

But see, the dragon
has eaten the princess
and the princess
has eaten the frog
who was the prince,
and as for the king,
he was in the worst of all
possible worlds,
he was just TERRIBLE.

So the prince
is inside the frog
who is inside the princess
who is inside the dragon

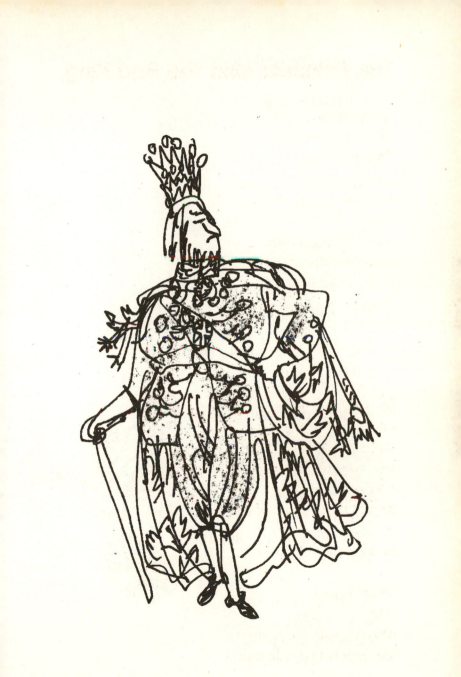

who is eyeing up the king
and
ONETWOTHREE!
has swallowed the king whole.

But the thing about a bad place
is you simply have to get out...

SO...

The princess walks out of the dragon,
just like that,
straight out through his mouth.
Then the princess opens her mouth
and out pops the frog,

who gives one great
BELCH
and out pops the prince.

But as for the king,
should we let him out,
let him walk out just like that?
Does the world need yet another bad king?

No, says the princess.
No, says the prince.
No, says the frog.

And do they live happily after,
along with the dragon
inside whom the king
is muttering with fury?

Do we want a good story
or do we want a bad one?

Would a bad story
be a good thing
or a bad thing?
I think we should think about it,
I think we should consider
the good things and the bad things
and let the dragon decide

as dragons sometimes do.

Rumpelstiltskin

Do you remember Rumpelstiltskin,
the tiny old man with great grey beard
who could weave gold out of straw
and did so for the miller's daughter?

Well, here is a list of Rumpelstiltskin's brothers:

Dumplingstiltskin
Crumpetstiltskin
Stumblingstiltskin
Jumperstiltskin
Plumplipsstiltskin
Crumpledstiltskin
Grumpystiltskin
Chumptripstiltskin
Mumpspillstiltskin
Gazumpstiltskin
and
Billy-ho!

Go catch Rumpelstiltskin.
Call him by his name.
See if he is in.

The Emperor's New Clothes

The emperor loves clothes.
The emperor has wardrobes
which he fills up with clothes,
so he has to buy more wardrobes
which he also fills up,
then another
and another.

And so it goes on.

One emperor,
hundreds of wardrobes,
thousands of clothes,
most of which he never wears,
just clothes
just wardrobes.

Why does he do it?

He wants to be the best-dressed emperor,
the best dressed emperor ever.
He looks at himself in the mirror
and says: *That's pretty smart,*
that's beautifully made,
that fits so well,
that's really elegant.

And yet it's not enough
because emperors can never have enough
or else they wouldn't be emperors.

Then come two tricksters,
two sly tricksters
who have tricked emperors,
who have made fortunes
by making things up
that never existed
and never will exist.

They invented a ship
that never sailed the ocean.
They invented a car
that has never seen the road.
They invented moons
on the far side of the moon.
They invented planets
no astronomer can find.
They can conjure air
out of thin air.

The emperor gets a message.

WE ARE FAMOUS TAILORS
THE WONDERS OF THE WORLD
WE WORK MIRACLES
OUR CLOTHES ARE BEYOND FABULOUS
WE ARE IN TOWN
COME AND VISIT.

The emperor is tempted,
so he sends down a messenger
to check out their work.

The messenger arrives
and the tailors tell him,

Our clothes are so special
you have to be a genius
a genius to see them

a genius to wear them
and as for our best work
only emperors can see them
only emperors can wear them
and only special emperors at that.

Here's a coat, they say.
What do you think?

The messenger doesn't see a coat.
He doesn't see anything
because there's nothing there to see,
nothing at all.
But no one wants to look stupid,
especially messengers,
certainly not messengers of the emperor.
So the messenger says,

It's magnificent
it's brilliant
it's stunning
it's genius

and he goes back to the emperor
and tells him the same thing.

Bring me the tailors! says the emperor.

The tailors appear,
wondrously courteous,
measure up the emperor,
coat, jacket, trousers,
frilly shirt and all.

Back in three days, they say.
They disappear for three days,
then they return.

The emperor puts on the clothes.
The emperor says nothing. Then,
What do you think? he asks all his messengers.

The messengers gulp.
The messengers think.
What's the right thing to say?

Magnificent, cries one.
Brilliant, bellows another.
Stunning, whispers a third.
Genius, whistles the fourth.

The emperor thinks
as he stands at the mirror
he looks pretty naked –
but cannot admit it
because if he did
he'd not be a genius,
an emperor of course,

but nothing really special.
So he says, **Yes,**
it is rather splendid,
just a bit tight perhaps
under the arms.

A *moment*, cry the tailors,
snipping the air, stitching the air
while the emperor holds up his arms.
Is that better now?

Yes, says the emperor,
infinitely better.

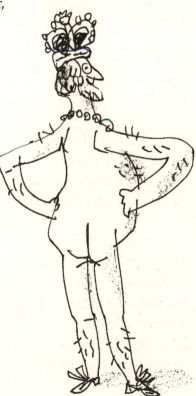

79

The next day is his birthday,
time for celebration
out in the streets,
out with the emperor's people.

But there in the crowds
is a five-year-old boy
who isn't a genius,
who isn't an emperor.

There's a joke somewhere here,
something about a birthday suit.

But somebody else can explain that.
All I know is

it was cold out in the street
and it was getting colder.

Sleeping Beauty

Sleeping Beauty
(what a cutie!)
slept a very long time
(far too long for this rhyme).

Then came a prince.

She's been awake since.

Hansel and Gretel

*My tale is done, there runs a mouse, whosoever
catches it may make himself a big fur cap out of it.*

There runs a mouse
with a story to tell
about two lost children.

Do we know their names?

Yes we do.
They are Hansel and Gretel,
whose parents left them in the forest
at a time of great hunger
when there was nothing to eat.

No ham, no cheese, no pickle,
no carrots, no potatoes,
no fizzy drinks. Nothing sweet
that certain people like to eat.

Hansel and Gretel,
brother and sister,
lost in the forest,
waiting for moonlight,
wandering at night
past wolves and bears
and lions and tigers

and terrible snakes
and dragons and spiders...

Brave children but hungry,
clever but tired, said the mouse,
until they came to a marvellous house.
A house made of food,
not just any old food,
the walls made of jammy dodgers,
the roof of jam doughnuts
and the windows of ice
flavoured with banana,
and they were so hungry
they started to eat it.

I wouldn't think of eating a house.
I live in dark corners and sometimes nip out
to grab what I can, then scuttle back in.
I'm a house mouse after all,
said the mouse, and went on with the story.

Just then, said the mouse, the witch scuttled out
with a charming smile, with the kindest of looks,
not the ugly witch you read of in books
but utterly gorgeous in a splendid white dress.
And she said to the children:

'You do look a mess.
You look far too thin.
You must be so hungry.
Why don't you come in?'

SO THE CHILDREN WENT IN.

But once inside the witch changed her looks
and looked pretty much like the witches in books
because, if you don't mind me giving advice,
not everything's good that at first sight looks nice.

(The mouse was the kind that liked to advise
and considered itself to be wary and wise.)

The children were trapped,
the witch started to beat them
but her real intention
was simply to eat them.
'You see this oven?
A gift from the coven.
Now you have seen it
I want you to clean it.
Get in,' said the witch.
'Get in or I'll make you.
I'm dying to bake you.'

Though Hansel and Gretel were small, said the mouse,
they were far from stupid.
They had a trick or two up their sleeve.

'We've never got into an oven before.
Will we fit through the oven door?
Can you show us how to do it?'

'Anyone can wriggle through it,' said the witch.
'It's easily big enough for you.
I will show you what to do.'

With that she opened the oven door
and squeezed in tight.
'Oh yes,' cried the children.
'We see. You're right.'
So saying, they slammed the door
And locked the witch in.
The witch burned.

Now there's a lesson to be learned,
the mouse explained.
Never get into the oven
unless the witch gets in there first.

What happened next?
What happened to the children?

Oh, they got rich
and lived happily ever after,
said the mouse,
looking remarkably like a big fur cap.

Supertailor!

There once was a tailor
who wasn't very clever
and no one praised him,
no one ever!

BUT ONE DAY...

He made a jam sandwich
and left it on the sill
while he worked on a belt
and carried on working and working, until...

FLIES!
SEVEN OF THEM!
ALL OVER THE JAM!

So he took the belt he was working on
and swatted all seven, seven at once.
(SPLAT! went the jam.)

That's pretty good,
seven at once
and never mind the jam.

And the tailor cried,

I am no dunce.

Never mind the jam,
I am a dragon-slayer, I am!
From now on no one calls me a failure!
I am Fly-killer, SUPERTAILOR!

And he wrote on his belt
SEVEN AT A BLOW.
But seven of *what*?
No one would ever know.
Seven sparrows?
Seven moles?
Seven fierce tigers?
Seven enormous trolls?

Nobody knew, but out he strode,
proud as a peacock, down the road.
Walking along, he came to a town
where the Giant was a pest.
And as soon as people saw his belt
they somehow thought, they somehow felt,
that when it came to Giant-killing
he would be by far the best.

Supertailor! people cried,
Save us from the Giant!
And the tailor replied,
You can be my very first client.
I will save you from the Giant.

And then he did, but how he did it
remained a secret because he hid it.
And so he went from town to town
wherever dragon-slayers were needed.
He took the job...
　　　　　　and he succeeded!

Shall I tell you the secret? Well, why not!
He had invented a neat fly-swat
that could kill at fifty paces,
while a Giant was doing up his laces,
having breakfast, or having a break.
Just one swat is all it would take.

Whether he ever killed seven at once, I don't
　　know,
but he would certainly have a go.

I'm SUPERTAILOR! he declared.
Bring out your dragons. Get prepared.
I am a superhero, I am.
Then he would SPLAT all seven like jam.

　　Such a tall tale could last for hours.
　　　　The lesson is: GET SUPERPOWERS!

91

The Pasta with the Pesto

Take your pasta,
add the pesto
(it is best to
press the pesto
in the pasta).
Now add peas to
both the pesto
and the pasta.
Try a tester
with a taster
but don't pester
your big sister
who can muster
her own pasta.
Lastly please to
pass the pasta
with the pesto,
and...
     hey presto!

A Flying Visit

Must go, says Mo
Must stay, says May
Must leave, says Eve
Have gone, says John
Am here, says Keir
Have tea, says Fee
How you? asks Prue
Quite well, says Nell
Must part, says Art
Must fly, says Guy
Must fly.

Creak Creak!

Time for presents
time for lights
time to stay up
late at nights
time for Mum
and Dad to sneak
mysterious boxes
in, *creak creak!*

Creak creak the stairs
and mutterings
and pilings up
and clutterings
and decking trees
with lights that blink
blue, green, yellow...
Time to think
of what's to come
not of what's gone.

*Merry Christmas
everyone!*

Afterglow

The magic lasts for days and days.
Everything glows, all the lights are on.

People's houses grow spectacular
With flashing bulbs and winking candles
And the shops are filled with jangling music
And the people behind the counters
Are wearing sparkling make-up and reindeer horns.

Just think if the world were always like this,
Every day dizzy and flashing and revolving
And there was snow, real or pretend,
And Christmas was for ever, without end!

And the quiet, the snuggling-up,
Was saved for one vast morning
That spread through the house
Like a kiss or good news.

GEORGE SZIRTES

is a widely acclaimed Hungarian-born British poet. He has won a variety of prizes for his work, including the T.S. Eliot Prize for his collection, *Reel*, and the 2013 CLPE Award for his children's collection, *In the Land of Giants*. His translations from Hungarian poetry, fiction and drama have also won numerous awards, including the translators' prize in the Man Booker International. George Szirtes lives in Wymondham, Norfolk.